Steel Masks

Poetry by

Joseph S. Salemi

ISBN-13: 978-0615608990

Cover art: Albrecht Dürer, *Das welsche Turnier* (1516)

White Violet Press
1840 West 220th St
Suite 300
Torrance, Calif. 90501

To Helen

uxori semper dilectissimae

Acknowledgments

Steel Masks (*The New Formalist*)
Criticism of Life (*Masquerade*)
The Stationmaster Speaks (*Chronicles*)
American Air Raid (*Trinacria*)
Villanelle for Sigmund Freud (*Formal Complaints*)
The Bones of the Armenians (*First Things*)
Mining Accident (*Raintown Review*)
To an Aging Countercultural Twit (*Nonsense Couplets*)
Time Capsule (*Chronicles*)
Sniper (*Dark Horse*)
The Gunnery Sergeant Speaks (*Measure*)
Genesis (*The HyperTexts*)
My Daughter's Garden (*Measure*)
Priamel for Writer's Block (*Victorian Violet*)
Military Funeral (*Victorian Violet*)
St. Anthony and the Demons (*Trinacria*)
Your Grandmother's Verse (*Lucid Rhythms*)
The Ossuary at Verdun (*Formal Complaints*)
The Sergeant's Warning (*Skirmishes*)
For Benson A. Koenig (*First Things*)
Suicide Bomber (*Measure*)
A Feminist Professor Lectures (*Masquerade*)
An Academy Painter Judges the Impressionists (*Masquerade*)
Épuration (*Lucid Rhythms*)
The Woman Who Froze (*Masquerade*)

Plus Ça Change... 1864-1954 (*Lucid Rhythms*)
Potpourri (*Victorian Violet*)
Rathskeller Girl (*Chronicles*)
The Psychopath Addresses the Ladies Auxiliary (*Trinacria*)
Charity's Gift (*Blue Unicorn*)

Table of Contents

Steel Masks

King Henri II of France was accidentally killed in 1559 during a festive tournament when he was lanced in the eye by Gabriel Montgomery, seigneur de Lorges, a member of his Garde Ecossaise. A young Italian nobleman named Luigi Corbinelli witnessed the event, and was so profoundly moved by it that he renounced the world and joined the Jesuit order.

The swirling pomp of ceremony, gold
And ermine, banners blazoned in vermilion—
Heraldic pennants waving in the sun
Float high above the lists and the pavilions.

The wedding day of France's royal daughter
Has packed Parisian streets with festive throngs,
While clanking weapons and the thrum of lutes
Contend with trumpets, bells, and brazen gongs.

The king is flushed, ebullient, in his prime—
A monarch at the pinnacle of pride.
His every gesture summons from the crowd
A roar of hoarse approval. Then there rides

Montgomery to the joust. His face is masked
In gleaming steel; he holds his ribboned lance
Level and ready for the playful tilt.
The lords and commons cheer as horses prance.

The Scotsman's lance-tip glances off the shield
King Henri holds at some ill-fated angle
And drives right through his visor. In one pass
The king is dead, his brains a bloody tangle.

A shock runs through the city, and then France,
Where death has entered like a silent thief.
A young Italian noble who had come
To take part in this wedding-turned-to-grief

Is stricken to the core. He cannot sleep.
All food is tasteless, every pleasure nil.
He thinks of Henri, vigorous and fit,
Dead for a silly, momentary thrill.

Returning home to Florence, he then deeds
All rights in his estate to a relation,
Presents himself to the Ignatian Order.
When asked, he gives this simple explanation:

"I saw King Henri speared straight through his mask
Of iron, by another masked in steel.
And at that moment I saw through the sham
Of life, and how it hides us from the Real.

We think our vizards tempered, well-wrought, proof—
But they are brittle masks that cannot blunt
The thrust that sends us down to that cold realm
For which life is a flimsy, pasteboard front."

Criticism of Life

The main end and aim of all our utterance, whether in prose or in poetry, is surely a criticism of life.

—Mathew Arnold, Preface to *Byron's Poetry* (1881)

Matthew Arnold, crashing bore,
Orotund loquacious snore,
Crafter of old Persian scenes,
Scourge of bourgeois Philistines,
Keeper of the gem-like flame,
Arbiter of praise and blame,
Parceller-out of reputations,
Fount of placid observations,
Child of Rugby's birchen rods,
Priest of England's household gods,
Champion of all that's grand,
Vatic voice of Dover's strand—
Teach what to criticize
When life has shrunk to pygmy size.

The Stationmaster Speaks

A railway system's all about routine—
Unchanging rhythms make the whole thing useful.
The scheduled stops are fixed, time in between
Kept to determined length, and a cabooseful
Of necessary plans is held on file
Lest anything untoward or strange transpire.
The passengers, on seats or in the aisle,
Pay fares that incrementally get higher.

So, as you see, uncertainty is banished.
Conductors punch your ticket, save the stub,
And synchronize their watches. Gone and vanished
All *contretemps* and glitches. Here's the rub:
The tracks are straight and smooth, embankments leveled.
Why should the world outside be so disheveled?

American Air Raid

America is the Great Satan.

—Ruhollah Khomeini

One night of moonless terror, great Lucifer's broad wings
Rose up in smoky billows from the flame of hellish things:
The pyres of the Ganges, the ovens of the camps,
The smokestacks of Chicago and the trashcans of the tramps.

They turned and swooped like falcons upon the victim earth—
Brought shadows of disease and grief, of destitution, dearth,
Of unexampled murder, atrocity full blown—
Whatever pain could touch us at the soul or at the bone.

They left behind them weeping, the groans of broken men,
The shrieking of the wounded at their mangled flesh. And then
The wings sank back to darkness, like adders to their holes,
Where devils are inured and deaf to screaming human souls,

And where no breath of music, no lilting plaint of lyres,
No harmony of voices from the archangelic choirs,
No seven spheres in concert, no chiming of a bell
Can break the mirthless silence at the icy core of hell.

Villanelle for Sigmund Freud

The seeds of grief are early sown
Deep in the cellars of the mind;
They promise harvest yet unknown.

A cache of poison at the bone,
Contagion in the fruit and rind—
The seeds of grief are early sown.

Whatever pain we may postpone,
Whatever scrap of joy we find—
They promise harvest yet unknown.

This is the knife our hearts must hone,
The whetstone bloodied as we grind;
The seeds of grief are early sown.

And with faces blank as stone
Three sisters spin the thread and wind;
They promise harvest yet unknown.

For what crime do we atone?
In what webs are we entwined?
The seeds of grief are early sown;
They promise harvest yet unknown.

The Bones of the Armenians

Son of man, can these bones live?

—Ezekiel, 37:3

Not the trump of Gabriel, nor the tumult
Stirred up by a clamorous resurrection
Can awaken bones from that desert nightmare's

        Prodigal torment.

Not the prayers from myriad begging voices,
Solemn penance chanted by dirging fathers
In atonement's chorus of expiation

        Cleanses the blood-guilt.

Neither screaming pleas of a gang-raped mother,
Nor the pistol shots to the heads of children
Rouse them out of somnolence. Nothing serves to

        Summon avengers.

Just the dumb remembrance and silent breathing
Of those few survivors who still can picture
1915's Golgotha, red with murder,

        Waiting for answers.

Mining Accident

A rumble as of shellfire ten leagues off
But closing in, the stale and foetid air;
The hacking of an aggravated cough,
A single lantern's red electric glare;

The stench of motors, overheated oil,
Hot metal, shorted wires, gasoline;
The rancid sweat of terror mixed with toil,
The pregnant creaking of a wooden beam.

Suddenly dense asphyxiating clouds
Of coal dust, soot and splinters, powdered grit;
Miasmic gases, thick as blackened shrouds,
Caught in your tears and mingled with your spit;

And then the thought that here is where you'll lie:
Five thousand feet away from air and sky.

To an Aging Countercultural Twit

At Woodstock you went walking in the nude,
But you were high on pot, and just a teen—
Your life is now more upscale and subdued,
And tinted with environmental green.

You still think Marx a genius, but not quite
As brilliant as Adorno or Marcuse;
Despite rheumatic damps, you will ignite
If someone sparks your old New Leftist fuse.

Fatally swift are time's extended wings—
So many sainted icons rose and fell!
Your heart yearns for those past—and passing—kings:
Daniel Ortega, Ho Chi Minh, Fidel.

Where are the marching Workers of the World?
Where are the barricades and surging crowds?
Where are the rocks and gasoline bombs hurled
Against policemen swathed in tear gas clouds?

Gone with the wind. Like *Rolling Stone* and Mao,
They've slipped into the dustbin of the past.
The only places that give solace now
Are Berkeley, North Korea, Cambridge Mass.

You've joined a health club, and you watch your weight.
Macrobiotic meals and exercise
May also undermine the bourgeois state
And work against the hegemonic lies.

Take vitamins, fruit juice, and lengthy hikes
But take them with a grain of salt. Perhaps
Organic foods and stationary bikes
Will not stave off the ultimate collapse.

Time Capsule

We filled it with the icons of this age:
A cellphone, condoms, iPod, and a beeper;
Viagra, vitamins, a sample page
Of cable TV listings, and the cheaper
Sort of costume jewelry. As for print,
A copy of the Sunday *New York Times*;
And just to give posterity a hint
Of grittiness, a list of all the crimes
Committed in the course of this past year;
The names of several starlets and their diets;
An advertisement for our home-brewed beer
And CDs of the latest urban riots.

So down it went, to wait for resurrection,
When how we lived shall come up for inspection.

Sniper

He lifts the rifle carefully, while Death
Sits like a patient uncle. Then he squeezes
The gently yielding trigger. Half a breath
Escapes him as the tensile mainspring eases.

A bullet sings, and finds its chosen place:
An intersection where taut spider thread
Marks a right angle on a human face—
His scope reveals a flagrant burst of red

Just for an instant. Motionless he waits
Ten calibrated seconds by his watch.
Unbroken silence. Turmoil dissipates.
Tonight the stock receives a single notch.

He draws the bolt back, and a glint of brass
Hops like a praying mantis on the grass.

The Gunnery Sergeant Speaks

The regulation Army automatic
Has solid heft, well balanced in the heel—
A complex interaction of blued steel,
With operation simple, but dramatic.

Push up the magazine until it catches:
The rasp is unmistakably distinct—
Metallic zip conjoined with the succinct
Snap of precise, machine-worked coupling latches.

With guns, the trick is thoughtful concentration.
Just rack the slide, and chamber in a round—
There is pure satisfaction in that sound:
The oiled click of perfect calibration.

And afterwards? Why, then you blast away.
At what or whom is not for me to say.

Genesis

Way back in the Jurassic, when the reptiles ruled the earth
All living creatures gave Tyrannosaurus Rex wide berth;
His jaws and his incisors were decisive in a fight—
No other being could survive his devastating bite.

This T. Rex was a nightmare from the deepest pit of hell;
His rule was total, absolute, and mercilessly fell.
He tore, he ripped, he slashed, he rent; his steps made *terra*
quake,
And when he roared his savage voice caused everyone to shake.

And yet around his monstrous feet, imbrued with blood and
gore,
There scurried little creatures that I doubt he even saw.
Or if he noticed, these small things occasionally served
To give Tyrannosaurus Rex a sampling of *hors d'oeuvres.*

These creatures were the mammals, an obscure and minor breed:
Warm-blooded little vertebrates whose infant young would feed
On milk from teats—a novelty in that egg-bearing time,
When almost everything was hatched in clutches or in slime.

And so it went for eons, and it never would have changed—
Tyrannosaurus ruled the roost; the mammals never ranged
Much wider than the forest floor, where they could always hide
In underbrush and foliage, and hope they'd not be spied.

Until one day an asteroid from some far distant source
Came crashing down into the earth with such stupendous force

It pulverized whole mountains, it evaporated seas;
It detonated with a heat unmeasured in degrees.

It generated tidal waves, and triggered seismic shocks—
It scorched the world with fire and it melted solid rocks.
It sent up in the atmosphere a cloud of cosmic dust
So choking and so toxic that the dinosaurs went bust.

The sun was blocked for years and years; the temperature soon dropped,
And reptiles with their stone-cold blood stood motionless and stopped.
Tyrannosaurus couldn't cope, and transformed into coal,
And all the other mega-beasts soon sank in the same hole.

When all was calm, who had survived? The mammals, to be sure—
They managed to get through the blast, to hang on and endure;
There wasn't any T. Rex now to cause dismay and fuss,
And so they leisurely evolved into the thing called us.

My Daughter's Garden

The earth was plowed and raked, the auger's holes
Spaced neatly. With her father standing near
She put each seedling in, and pressed it down.
I thought *With beetles, cutworms, and the moles*
There's little chance for growth. And then a sheer
Flash of terror struck. Will her hopes drown
Not just this spring, but for all time as well?
Are childhood's gardens anterooms to hell?

She watered them. And I asked, as she poured,
How tall will flowers grow? Will they reach far?
So high, she said, her finger pointing toward
The woodshed's slanting roof of tin and tar.
And all at once a flock of sparrows soared
Skyward like arrows arching to a star.

Priamel for Writer's Block

As the dawn pursues the starlight,
As the river seeks the sea,
As the east wind scours leaf-fall,
So I chase my fantasy.

As the starling pecks at blindworms,
As the falcon swoops to cruise,
As the owl preys on field mice,
So I hunt the vagrant muse.

And when twilight finds me helpless
I abhor the chaste, blank page
While it smiles in mocking laughter
At my wordless, stifled rage.

Military Funeral

The muffled roll of drums, the folded flag;
Three volleys from bolt-actions, sharp and crisp;
The clink of cartridge casings, and a wisp
Of bluish smoke. Then Taps begins its drag
Of lengthened notes—a melismatic wail
That seems to last forever. Next the scrape
Of boots as guardsmen exit, while black crepe
Billows beside the bier, an unlashed sail
Loose in autumnal breeze. The moment hits
The widow, whose composure starts to break.
She cannot hold back sobs; her shoulders shake.
Except for her, the grief-numbed family sits
As if held in suspended animation,
Deaf to the murmured "…from a grateful nation."

Saint Anthony and the Demons

*For when demons come they approach us in a form
corresponding to the state in which they discover us, and adapt
their delusions to the condition of mind in which they find us.*

—Athanasius of Alexandria, *Life of Saint Anthony*, 42

Nothing but sand and rocks and thorny shrubs
And heat so torrid that a foetid tomb
Seems like a royal chamber—this alone
I take as my allotted share of earth.
Friends and family? I can barely dream
Their visages, much less how we once laughed
And wasted time in pointless talk and games.
My throat and lips are parched by constant prayer—
Other than prayer and windsongs, only silence.

Then they come. Like moisture-laden clouds
That roll in waves of thunder overhead
And seem dark billows of a hostile sea
They come. I could not stop them if I tried.
Sometimes it is a woman's shapely form
Breathing the heavy scent of untouched fruit
And smiling welcome and solicitude;
Or else a young priest, asking for advice;
A fellow anchorite perplexed by doubts;
And now and then a sickly Negro child.
He alone is truthful, for he says
I am the spawn of whoredom, and runs off
As soon as I invoke the name of Christ.

At first they reason with me, and attempt
To demonstrate my life's cold bitterness.
After that, the mockery begins:
Sarcastic jibes, derision, obloquy,
Cruel mirth at my drab rags and unwashed skin,
The insolence of spirits toward mere flesh.
But this you must expect. I am a man,
And they can break our human fortitude
Only by plaguing tissue, blood, and bone.

Demons intuit in a flash, and know
Without the bovine ox-tread we call thought:
The tedious amassing of small facts,
Laborious deductions, inference,
The clumsy give-and-take of dialectic,
The clatter of our syntax as it strives
To fix in language what our wits have grasped—
All of this is trivia and trash
To demons, who are intellect alone.
And yet to speak with us, they must use words,
Stooping to our base level just to make
Their impudent suggestions understood.
Any rejection hurts them in their pride,
And that is when the lying masks are dropped.

I will tell you all that I have seen:
Troops of soldiers armed, high court officials;
Scorpions, hyaenas, hungry wolves
Bulls and lions, panthers, crocodiles;
Robbers, madmen, acolytes, and whores;
Satan himself with nostrils belching flame—
They all appeared at one time or another.
There is a single rule to follow here:
No matter what you see, ask *Who are you?*
And why do you disturb a hermit's prayer?
This unmans demonic arrogance—
They see that there is substance in your spine
Backed up by our Savior and the Saints.
If you were to show fear or hesitation
All would be lost as they made tight their circle
And pressed advantage, jackals that they are.

The final stage is undisguised assault.
In my case it begins with one sharp slap
Across the cheek, then escalates to more.
When they are finished, I am badly bruised,
My mouth awash in blood, my eyes and lips
Swollen with pain. I cannot hear or see
And yet I know God's grace has beaten them.
Once they have vented fury by these blows
Their failure is explicit. I can sleep
And wait to see what new lies they concoct
When they return. Return they always do.

Such is my daily torment, but recall
That Christ Himself went out into the desert
And faced the tests of Satan. God's own Son
Was tried and questioned by the Common Foe.
Do not take the eremitic path
For solitude alone. I guarantee
Even in wastes and wilderness remote
No one escapes an all-observing Hell.

Your Grandmother's Verse

She writes it with a quill pen, so they say,
On cream-smooth vellum (paper she refuses).
A photo of three granddaughters at play
Sits on her desk to supplement the Muses.

Her subjects? Cats, and apple pies, and toys;
Quilted covers, macramé, and knitting;
A nest of robin's eggs, the happy noise
Of birthday party games, and sparrows flitting.

And all throughout this theme park of contentment,
This playland of the placid and the cute,
Not one word of corruption or resentment,
Of competition, hatred, or dispute
Or anything that hints a human life
Might know the wolf-howl, or the jagged knife.

The Ossuary at Verdun

I am moved by fancies that are curled
Around these images, and cling:
The notion of some infinitely gentle
Infinitely suffering thing.

    —T. S. Eliot, *Preludes*

Obedient bones, remembering
Through bayonets and tangled wire
Some infinitely gentle thing.

New splinters turn up every spring,
Confettied by the guns' brute fire—
Obedient bones, remembering

(While Mort Homme closed its deadly ring)
How each lived moment would inspire
Some infinitely gentle thing

Before the order came to fling
One's flesh upon that hideous pyre—
Obedient bones, remembering

La Voie Sacrée would daily bring
Fresh faces to the trench's mire:
Some infinitely gentle thing.

Around these shards the specters cling
All gathered in a mystic choir—
Obedient bones, remembering
Some infinitely gentle thing.

The Sergeant's Warning

When tossing grenades, you must follow some rules;
Neglect even one and you're toast—
You treat these devices like playthings for fools
And you'll exit the field as a ghost.

First take out the pin with a single swift yank—
Don't hesitate, dawdle, or linger.
The bomblet is not a respecter of rank
So use your most powerful finger.

The lever's released in a spring-driven flip
That makes a most audible plinking;
That sound is your cue, so be sure of your grip
On your nerves, and your wits, and your thinking.

Count slowly to four, and then fling from your hand
(Long arcs give your throws an advantage).
Don't wait to observe where the damned thing may land—
Drop down and lie flat as a bandage!

With luck you'll hit something or someone. Who knows?
You might even pick up a medal.
But staying alive when a pineapple blows
Is something for which I would settle.

For Benson A. Koenig (1912-1997)

Battery A, 10th AART Battalion, US Army
North Africa and Italy, 1942-44

Those last three days, reciting from memory
Cicero and Vergil…you could quote
Long passages of Latin poetry.
It left us stunned. The only antidote
To poison in your flesh was blessèd words.
No other good thing comforted you when
Pulsating life, just like a flock of birds,
Gathered its wings to fly. The deaths of men
Can be as silent as the moon's eclipse,
Spectrally speechless as fields after battle,
Loud as the riven sky's apocalypse
With thundering noise—or mindless as a rattle.
Benson, your answer to encroaching dark
Was language and its lustrous, flaming spark.

Suicide Bomber

A jacket packed with gelignite sewn in
With carpet nails, ball bearings, shards of glass—
Two detonator caps and striking pin
Taped to his back, and wired up to pass
Beneath his groin, while resting in his pocket
A simple circuit switch awaits his thumb.
Around his neck, he wears a golden locket
That holds a sacred text of life to come.

He thinks of peoples, nations, tribes, and races—
Those networks of identity and rage:
The fallen friends, the unavenged, whose faces
Gaze and applaud as if he were on stage.

And yet it's he who triggers—all alone—
The flame-red sunburst of his blood and bone.

A Feminist Professor Lectures on
The Rape of the Lock

This is a patriarchal, sexist piece:
The lock's a helpless, victimized, ideal
Gynal trophy (like the Golden Fleece)
That masculinist enterprise must steal.
Persons without false consciousness should feel
Outrage at how Belinda is oppressed
Both by the Baron, and the author's zeal
For perfumes, *billets-doux*, and all the rest
Of hierarchy's baubles. Women dressed
In corsets, bustles, petticoats, and stays!
Such voyeuristic cameos suggest
Gender restriction more than beauty's praise.
As for the forfex—well, now there you are:
It's phallomorphic, just like Freud's cigar.

An Academy Painter Judges the Impressionists

Impressionists? Their palettes are ablaze
With upstart colors heretofore unseen.
The lack of expert drafting makes for haze
And blurring in their polychromic scheme:
Puce, lemon, antique rose, and tangerine;
Cinnabar shading into umber hints;
Streaks of a velvet peridotal green
Speckled with azure flecks and ruby tints.
Sienna strokes are stabbed with yellow glints
Of golden fire, while a violet hue
Bleeds into ochre patches; orange sprints
In flashes across lilac and soft blue.
Not unexpected—once you banish line
Color runs riot like an unpruned vine.

Épuration

On the Greek isle of Tilos are the ruins of the sanctuary
of Pythian Apollo. Over them has been built the Church
of the Archangel Michael.

Now rot here on the earth that nourishes men. No longer
will you live to be an evil mischief to mortals.

  —Homeric Hymn to Apollo

Saint Michael, God's own musketeer,
Commander of angelic hosts;
Saint Michael of the lucent spear
Too glorious to be dimmed by boasts;

Hold back the hordes of this sick age
That seek our blood on every side—
The Mongols of our lust and rage,
The Persians of our pampered pride.

May your lance pierce the inward parts
Of what drives our diseased decline—
Like Phoebus, fill the beast with darts
And leave it in putrescent slime.

Let your sword swing and dole out death
In one immense and lethal arc
To all whose leprous, tainted breath
Infects the light and plagues the dark.

Like Trojans, may their throats be cut
By Achilleus, lost to hope—
Or let them, like the suitors' sluts,
Dance strangled on a laundry rope.

Let them lie in mounded pyres
Awaiting the all-cleansing flame—
Let them belch, in those last fires,
The stench of their forgotten name.

And then, Saint Michael, Like-to-God,
Stand watch against vindictive night,
Lest gore from your chastising rod
Bring back, unseen, the venomed blight.

The Woman Who Froze

She never knew a time she was not scared
From childhood right up to the present hour.
Her very steps were taken as if dared

Against some awful sanction that held power
Over her blood and marrow. Every word
She spoke was hushed, and shadowed with a cower.

None could convince her that it was absurd
To be enslaved by fearful hesitation,
So when she moved, the air was barely stirred—

At parties, in the swirl of conversation,
She sat apart, unnoticed and alone,
Nursing a self-sequestered isolation.

More and more she wished she were a stone:
Immovable, impassive, and unflinching
Before the rainfall's tears and wind's soft groan.

And so her life proceeded, slowly inching
Toward the conclusion that this trend prefigured:
Her habits became dispositions, clinching

Her fate, as sure as filth will foul a pig yard.
Uncertainties took root and grew like weeds.
They choked her shut, until she was a niggard

Not of mere words, but even simple deeds—
She barely moved a terror-frozen hand
To satisfy her elemental needs.

Her relatives did not quite understand;
The doctors were all helpless to advise—
It seemed as if some nameless malice planned

To clamp her motionless within a vise
Made from two jaws of hesitation paired
Like iron sentries at her captive sides.

Plus Ça Change… 1864-1954

At night my father brought back home the change
From his store's till, to sort and count and roll.
A simple task, and well within the range
Of childhood's skill. There was a heavy bowl
Where pennies went, and I would get the chance
To work my will. I made small stacks of them
So that they might be counted at a glance,
And then the thrill—one penny, like a gem,
Stood out from all the others, worn but thick,
While on it still the coin quite clearly bore
Its minting date, as plain as any brick—
A year to spill blood: 1864.

Nine decades it was warmed by hand and purse,
But warfare's chill persisted, getting worse.

Potpourri

Take leaves at first, curled crisp by autumn's cold—
Crush them to crumbly powder in a tray
To make a simple palette of decay
In varied tints of brown and red and gold.
Next flower petals, multicolored, bold
In stark chromatic contrasts—dry and bray
Them in a mortar till you cannot say
Which shade is which. Then choose a jar to hold
This mix of leaf and petal. Stir it well.
Put in dried leaves of mint, of basil, sage;
Add lavender and lilac, eglantine—
The lily, rue, and camphor's pungent smell.
Seal up the jar, and simply let it age—
The alchemy of death will work unseen.

Rathskeller Girl

Six steins, foam-flowing, three in either palm
She carries to our table, like first fruits:
Oktoberfest beer, smoother than the balm
Of Gilead, and more bracing. She salutes
Us with a smile and nod, as if she knew
We'd ask for refills soon enough. And yes,
The pungent crispness of that autumn brew
Begs for another round. Her *dirndl* dress
Swirls in a rush of orders. Presently
She brings more keg-fresh gold, heads yet to settle.
Again, her single-handed grip holds three,
As if the steins were lighter than a petal.
We try to mutter thanks; our German fails.
Her wink suggests *I know the needs of males.*

The Psychopath Addresses the Ladies Auxiliary of the Mental Ward

*When an inner situation is not made conscious, it
appears outside as fate.*

   —C.G. Jung

Physician, heal thyself.

   —Luke 4:23

Ladies, cease your mindless chatter
Lest I take a club and shatter
Your thick skulls and leave you bleeding
On the ground, alive but needing
Paramedical attention.
All your squawking and dissension
Makes me prone to savage violence.
Hold your tongues, and maintain silence.

That's much better. Doctor Kaiser
(Erstwhile head and supervisor
Of our little ward of loonies)
Has been transferred to the boonies.
Why you ask? Well, let me fill you
In on something. This'll kill you:
He's developed a psychosis
Of his own. The diagnosis
Isn't good. The guards have strapped him
To a gurney, and they've tapped him

For electroshocks and dousing,
And he'll get a thorough sousing
With the psychotropic potions
Used to quell untamed emotions.

If poor Kaiser shows improvement
(That is, if his speech and movement
Show the slurred and sluggish stupor
That's expected in our group or
Other medicated crazies)
He will join us. Though the days he's
Wasted as a sane physician
Now are gone, he'll share our mission:
Bearing witness, by his raving,
That the world's not worth the saving;
Testifying, by his drooling,
That the mind's immune to schooling;
Proving, by his unwiped feces,
That we are a helpless species.

Think of the prestige we're gaining—
A man of Kaiser's depth and training
Shares in the bizarre diseases
He once treated! Madness seizes
A brilliant mind, whose fine discerning

Sinks into a fevered burning;
A clinician's skill in observation
Polluted to hallucination!

Well, that's what I had to tell you.
Dinner's coming—there's the bell. You
Ought to set now, if you're able,
A place for Kaiser at the table.

Charity's Gift

When Jesus therefore saw His mother and the
disciple standing by whom He loved, He said
unto His mother: Woman behold thy son! *Then*
said He to the disciple: Behold thy mother! *And*
from that hour the disciple took her into his own
home.

   John 19: 26-27

Pinioned here, I look downwards to see
My mother weeping in unfettered grief
Her heart transfixed by swords, beholding Me
Hang from this branch like autumn's final leaf.

Disciple John—how much more than the rest
My soul smiles on him in completest love!
Mother and friend, by misery oppressed,
Huddle and hunch together. Raised above

This scene of bleeding spirits, I can make
No sign of recognition or concern
Except to speak out from My wooden stake
And give them to each other, for I yearn

To show the world how *caritas* unties
The bond of blood and flesh, and doing so,

Entwines a new knot even as it dies.
I bid you, *mater dolorosa,* go

And seek Me in the lambs that I hold dear:
The captives ransomed by My bitter cup—
For through this gift I make love's mandate clear:
Go wash each other's wounds, and bind them up.

About the Author

Joseph S. Salemi has published poems, translations, essays, reviews, and scholarly articles in over one hundred journals throughout the United States, Great Britain, and Canada. His published scholarship has touched upon writers as diverse as Chaucer, Machiavelli, Bembo, Castiglione, Blake, Kipling, Crane, Henley, Ernest Dowson, H.H. Munro, Willa Cather, and William Gaddis. His previous books of poetry are *Formal Complaints, Nonsense Couplets, Masquerade, The Lilacs on Good Friday,* and *Skirmishes.* He is a recipient of a Herbert Musurillo Scholarship, a Lane Cooper Fellowship, an N.E.H. Fellowship, the 1993 Classical and Modern Literature Award, and was a four-time finalist for the Howard Nemerov Prize. He is a monthly commentator and essayist for the on-line journal *The Pennsylvania Review,* and the editor and publisher of TRINACRIA. Salemi teaches in the Department of Classical Languages at Hunter College, C.U.N.Y. He is the grandson of the Sicilian poet and translator Rosario Previti (1882-1967).

MN, S
Presentation
by Author

1.⁵⁰